Flute Songs

Easy Familiar Classics with Orchestra

Jeffrey Zook, Flute

Stuttgart Festival Orchestra
Emil Kahn, Conductor

T0066231

To access audio visit:
www.halleonard.com/mylibrary

Enter Code
3225-3686-3196-0525

ISBN 978-1-59615-289-2

Music Minus One

EXCLUSIVELY DISTRIBUTED BY

HAL•LEONARD®

Visit Hal Leonard Online at
www.halleonard.com

Contact Us:
Hal Leonard
7777 West Bluemound Road
Milwaukee, WI 53213
Email: info@halleonard.com

In Europe, contact:
Hal Leonard Europe Limited
42 Wigmore Street
Marylebone, London, W1U 2RN
Email: info@halleonardeurope.com

In Australia, contact:
Hal Leonard Australia Pty. Ltd.
4 Lentara Court
Cheltenham, Victoria, 3192 Australia
Email: info@halleonard.com.au

CONTENTS

AIR ON A "G STRING"

from the Orchestral Suite No. 3 in D major, BWV1068

Johann Sebastian Bach
(1685-1750)

MINUET IN G

Arranged from Minuet for Piano in G, WoO10/2

Ludwig Van Beethoven
(1770-1827)

TRÄUMEREI

arranged for Flute & Orchestra from 'Kinderszenen,' op. 15, no. 7

Robert Schumann
(1810-1856)

MMO 3313

SERENATA
adapted from 'Schwanengesang,' D957, no. 4: 'Ständchen'

Franz Schubert
(1797-1828)

CAVATINE

Op. 85, No.3

Joachim Raff
(1822-1882)

Larghetto, quasi andantino

MINUET

Arranged from Divertimento No. 17 in D major, KV320b (KV334)

W.A. Mozart
(1756-1791)

Trio (slightly faster)

Menuetto D.C. al Fine

BERCEUSE
arranged from the opera 'Jocelyn'

Benjamin Godard
(1849-1895)

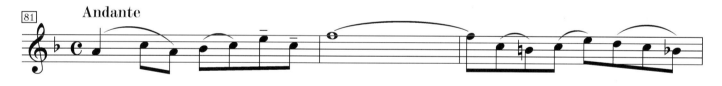

HUMORESQUE

arranged from the Humoresque No. 7 for piano, op. 101, no. 7

Antonín Dvořák
(1841-1904)

Poco lento grazioso

Un più mosso

HUNGARIAN DANCE NO. 5

arranged from Hungarian Dance No. 5 for Piano Duet, WoO 1/5

Johannes Brahms
(1833-1897)

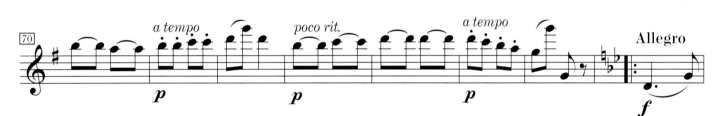